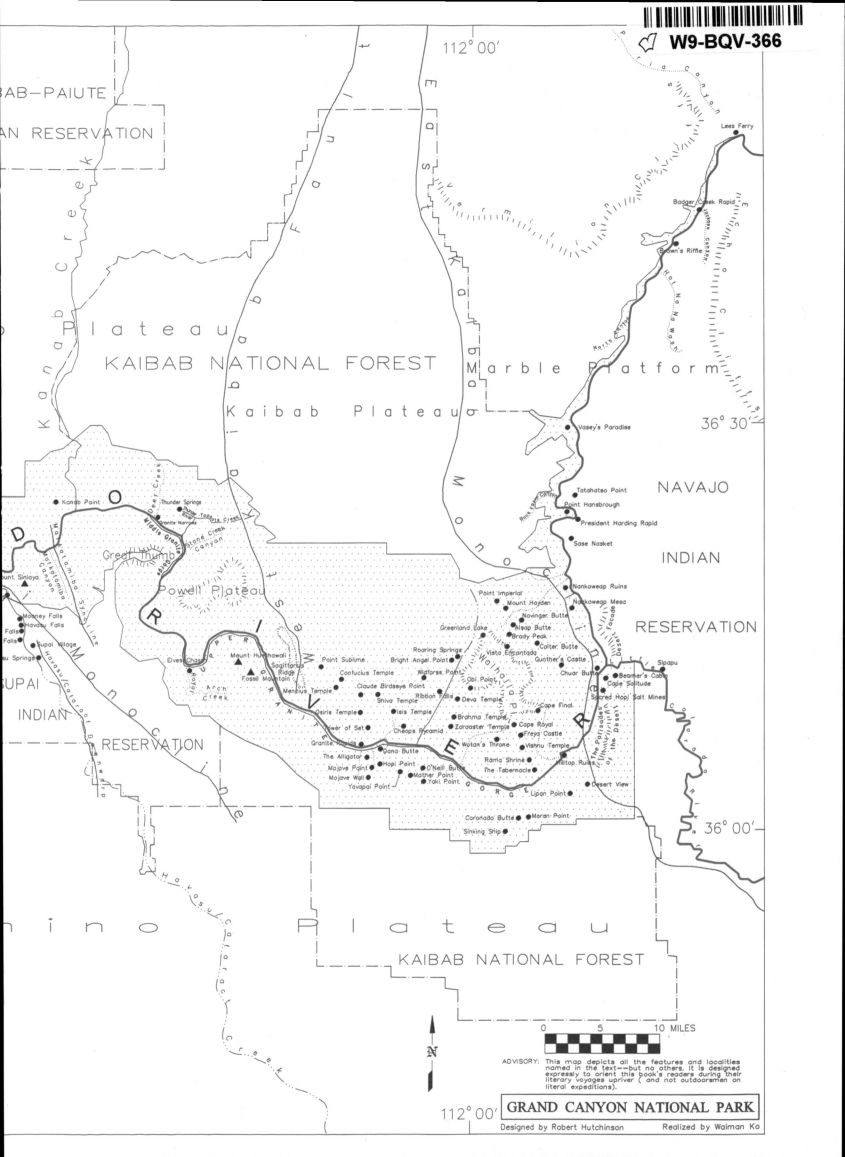

GRAND CANYON
NATIONAL PARK

A PHOTOGRAPHIC NATURAL HISTORY

WITH TEXT BY ROBERT HUTCHINSON
FEATURING THE PHOTOGRAPHY OF

WILLARD CLAY

CARR CLIFTON

KATHLEEN NORRIS COOK

JACK W. DYKINGA

JEFF FOOTT

JEFF GNASS

FRED HIRSCHMANN

DAVID MUENCH

MARC MUENCH

STEVE MULLIGAN

WILLIAM NEILL

RANDY A. PRENTICE

JAMES RANDKLEV

TOM TILL

LARRY ULRICH

BROWNTROUT PUBLISHERS
SAN FRANCISCO

INTRODUCTION

BOOKS on the Grand Canyon take their readers down the Colorado River.

Of course, down. The river definitely flows down, as John Wesley Powell in 1869 and the 22,000 river runners who floated the Canyon last year could all attest. Nobody cavils at the convention that fixes position in the Inner Gorge of the Grand Canyon by reference to the "River Mile" distance downstream from Lees Ferry, the zero-point in Glen Canyon National Recreation Area where river runners "put in" and below which the walls of the Grand Canyon make their modest first appearance. Only a twit would contest the assignment of the left bank to the South Rim.

What perversity could drive a Grand Canyon book upriver?

There are historical precedents for running the Canyon upriver. Twelve years before Powell's first expedition to the Grand Canyon, Joseph Christmas Ives, in fulfillment of his commission to ascertain the head of navigation on the Colorado River, chugged upstream 350 miles from its delta in the Gulf of California almost to the present site of Hoover Dam before cracking up his steamboat. Indomitable Lieutenant Ives continued on foot as far upstream as the Little Colorado River, along the way christening the "Big Cañon" (promoted to "Grand" by Captain Powell). Ives' upstream limit of navigability was dramatically extended in 1960, when Jon Hamilton—a New Zealander with an obstinately antipodean sense of direction—piloted three jet boats invented by his father in the only full uprun of the Grand Canyon.

Less exotic organisms have made the trip upriver more casually. Numerous low-desert species such as the Gila monster, the Joshua tree, and the blackbrush shrub have slipped through the western aperture of the Grand Canyon at Mile 278 and migrated upriver far from their homegrounds in the Mojave and Sonoran Deserts.

Inanimate bodies too waft into the depths of the Grand Canyon from the low desert to the west. Plunging down 6,000 feet of elevation along some rim-to-river transects, the Grand Canyon is as deep as an inverted mountain range. Elevation, rather than air-density stratification as in lesser valleys, controls the gross temperature gradient up the walls of the Grand Canyon. Temperature varies inversely with elevation. At lower elevations within the Grand Canyon, a tentacle of dry, hot air wends in from the Mojave Desert, ceaselessly groping the wet bottom.

Other fluid bodies can, under special circumstances, back upstream as well. At its high water mark of 1221 feet, Lake Mead (post-1935 artifact of Hoover Dam) sticks its river-choking tongue forty miles up the Grand Canyon. Six times in the last 1.2 million years, episodic lava flows into the Inner Canyon have built natural dams higher than Hoover Dam. One of these lava dams, three times higher than Hoover, backed its lake from Mile 179 all the way up the Grand Canyon and into Utah.

Still another kind of upriver movement is now held to be responsible for the very inception of that most animating of inanimate bodies in the Grand Canyon—our modern Colorado River. Until five million years ago, the ancestral lower and upper Colorado Rivers were separate and independent entities. The lower Colorado River had come into being very recently to drain the geologically young basin-range lowland southward into the newly-opened Gulf of California. The more venerable upper Colorado River ancestor drained the geologically adolescent Rocky Cordillera and Colorado Plateau southward in its upper reaches but then wheeled around out of what is now the middle of the Grand Canyon to empty inland to the northwest. An immature, hydraulically disequilibrated river seeks equilibrium by energetically cutting the head of its valley back into the source-upland. By such headward erosion, the lower Colorado River one fine day five million years ago breached the divide between the ancestral segments, blindsided the ancestral upper Colorado River where it turned northwest, and captured it.

This act of upriver piracy marked the inception not only of the modern Colorado River but also of the Grand Canyon. The modern Colorado's traction load has chipped a trench a mile deep through the Kaibab Dome between Miles 77 and 143, exposing in the Upper and Middle Granite Gorges the 1.7 billion-year-old metamorphic rocks of the Vishnu Complex at the crystalline core of the Dome.

Today's spectator standing on the Kaibab Limestone caprock at Bright Angel Point on the North Rim who looks south ten miles across the Canyon to the Kaibab Limestone capping the South Rim will observe that the latter is distinctly lower. This difference in elevation between stratigraphically equivalent points, measuring a thousand feet, reflects a line-of-sight laid down the dip of the southern flank of the Kaibab Dome. In vain, however, would our lynx-eyed spectator pore over the 5,700-foot-high Canyon walls for any remnant of the course followed by the ancestral upper Colorado River prior to the big hijack. To trace that bygone course, his gaze must bend skyward.

The ancestral upper Colorado River skittered around a shallow arcuate "racetrack" formed by the upturned edges of the Kaibab Dome's partially-eroded outer shells of sedimentary rock. Because erosion has since obliterated these soft Mesozoic outer shells, the phantom of the ancestral upper Colorado River perches high above today's rim. After banking the "racetrack" turn on the Dome's southern flank, the ancestral upper Colorado River ambled away leisurely to the northwest across the Arizona Strip.

The river was conducted along this northwest passage by a strike-valley. Erosional processes had notched out an array of northwest-trending strike-valleys at right angles to the gentle northeast dip of the region's strata as they descended from the erstwhile Mogollon Highlands to the south. Drainage in such northwest-trending strike-valleys has been preserved in exceptional cases to the present day in the Grand Canyon region by unusual stratigraphic controls (as in the case of the Little Colorado River) or structural controls (as in the case of the Cataract/Havasu Creek).

As the front of the extensional tectonic province of the basin-range advanced implacably from the south and west and sapped the foundations of the Mogollon Highlands, however, the northeastward tilt of the Grand Canyon region righted itself by degrees. The immemorial northwestward drainage suffered progressive enfeeblement and disruption. Its watery prize was ripe for the vigorous new invader from the west.

From the fateful moment that the westward-probing upstart river from the lowlands captured the debilitated river on the plateau, the profound potential energy difference in the base levels of these two ancestral segments drove the incision of the Grand Canyon into the southwestern Colorado Plateau. The rate of incision, accelerated by synchronous uplift of the Colorado Plateau, was spectacularly fast. The Colorado River effectively attained grade in the Grand Canyon by 1.2 million years ago; further incision of the Inner Gorge has been negligible. The locus of most active erosion has shifted away from the Colorado River canyon and up the tributary canyons as they gobble headward into the enclosing plateaux.

The Grand Canyon of the Colorado River is not, as sometimes trumpeted, a classic monument to uniformitarian processes operating over fathomless reaches of time. In truth, the Grand Canyon roared into life just recently as the issue of a random coupling of rivers.

A practical guidebook for Grand Canyon river runners that proceeded upriver would be hooted off the shelves as counter-intuitive nonsense. Yet why should boatmen's bias constrain a photo-book for those four million visitors (and countless non-visitors) to the Grand Canyon who each year do not run the river? Grand Canyon boatmen "take out" at Mile 225. Grand Canyon photo-books usually "take out" around Mile 179. By implication, the westernmost Grand Canyon is de trop—a superfluous coda to the main event so excellently savored from the drive-in panorama points overlooking the eastern Grand Canyon.

We have seen, however, that the story of the birth of the modern Colorado River and the consequent making of the Grand Canyon hinges critically in the west. A photo-book on the Grand Canyon that heads upriver appeals subtly to geodynamic intuition even as it defies simple gravity.

We propose to "put in" at Mile 278 and muscle our way upstream through successive segments of the Grand Canyon defined by the morphological style of the side canyons: the Esplanade (Miles 278-143), Kaibab (143-77), Chuar (77-53), and Marble Canyon (53-0) segments.

As we prepare now to probe the mouth of the Grand Canyon, look sharp! We are crossing the jagged frontier between warring tectonic provinces. Hear that subaudible rumble? A nearby mountain lion, maybe. Or maybe the kachina of that insensibly slow war of clashing rock that has conjured the Grand Canyon into being.

—Robert Hutchinson
April, 1995
Garrison, New York

GRAND CANYON NATIONAL PARK

A PHOTOGRAPHIC NATURAL HISTORY

Text ©1995 Robert Hutchinson

Photography ©1995
Willard Clay
Carr Clifton
Kathleen Norris Cook
Jack W. Dykinga
Jeff Foott
Jeff Gnass
Fred Hirschmann
David Muench
Marc Muench
Steve Mulligan
William Neill
Randy A. Prentice
James Randklev
Tom Till
Larry Ulrich

All rights reserved under International and Pan-American Copyright Conventions. No part of this book may be reproduced in any form or by any electronic or mechanical means without permission in writing from the publisher.

Published by
BROWNTROUT PUBLISHERS
P.O. BOX 280070
SAN FRANCISCO, CA 94128-0070
Printed by Dai Nippon, Hong Kong

Pages 2–3
CONFUCIUS TEMPLE, LOOKING SOUTHEAST FROM POINT SUBLIME (SUNSET, SEPTEMBER).
PHOTOGRAPH BY JEFF GNASS
Pages 4–5
PINYON PINE AND UTAH JUNIPER ON LIMESTONE SPIRES OF THE NORTH RIM, LOOKING FROM THE NORTH KAIBAB TRAIL (MORNING FOG).
PHOTOGRAPH BY JACK W. DYKINGA
Page 6–7
WINTER CLIFFS, SOUTH RIM.
PHOTOGRAPH BY WILLIAM NEILL

LIBRARY OF CONGRESS CATALOGING-IN-PUBLICATION DATA

Hutchinson, Robert, 1951 –
   Grand Canyon National Park : a photographic natural history / with text by Robert Hutchinson : featuring the photography of Willard Clay . . . [et al.].
      p.   cm.
   1. Natural history—Arizona—Grand Canyon National Park. 2. Natural history—Arizona—Grand Canyon National Park—Pictorial works. 3. Nature photography—Arizona—Grand Canyon National Park. 4. Grand Canyon National Park (Ariz.)—Pictorial works. I. Clay, Willard. II. Title.
QH105.A65H87 1995   95-26460
508.791'32'0222—dc20   CIP

THE MOUTH

JOSHUA TREE, GRAND WASH CLIFFS (April). The Joshua tree, growing up to 40 feet high, is the tallest of the yuccas. The tree's leathery foliage and crooked branches put sunstricken Mormon pioneers in mind of Joshua in his armor pointing the way to their Promised Land. A fine forest of Joshua trees grows around Pearce Ferry, only a few miles past Mile 278 in the Grand Wash Trough. A member of the Lower Sonoran botanical zone, the Joshua tree has infiltrated the western Grand Canyon.

PHOTOGRAPH BY TOM TILL

UNEASILY, we eye the huge raptorial birds suspended overhead on thermal drafts lifting off cliffs fired by the desert sunset. Our little party threads a jumble of limestone blocks on the inside bank of the big river where it churns red out of a curved slot in the cliffs. We file warily onto a beach inside the curve. A mountain lion raises its dripping muzzle and pads off sulkily into the gathering shadows. Dropping our packs at the river's edge and slinging our weapons, we scramble up into the forest to gather firewood. Then the stench hits us.

We follow our desert-scrubbed nostrils and wry grins to a cave at the foot of the tenebrous cliffs. We heap juniper boughs in the entrance and light them. The shaggy silhouette of a troglodyte heaves behind the wall of flame. Out topples a fragrantly smoking beast. As the giant ground sloth rears up with a grimace of torpid rage, our glinting spearpoints bristle around her.

Did some such unequal contest at Mile 275 mar our debut in the Grand Canyon of Arizona eleven thousand years ago? Well, not on the available archeological evidence from the Grand Canyon, which has yielded no radiocarbon ages older than about four thousand years. Yet tons of paleontological evidence from the Grand Canyon, taken together with archeological evidence of the presence of Desert Culture nomadic hunter-gatherers in the Mojave-Sonoran Desert some ten thousand years ago, lends a measure of plausibility to the vignette.

The grim rampart of rock that daunted our hypothetical Paleo-Indian band as they forayed upstream along the Colorado River out of their customary hunting range and into the mouth of the Grand Canyon is today called the Grand Wash Cliffs. These cliffs comprise the scarp of the Grand Wash Fault, which defines the tectonic boundary in Arizona between the uplifted Colorado Plateau and the downthrown Basin and Range Province.

The Grand Wash Fault initiated 17 million years ago to accommodate the Tertiary extensional deformation that has carved out the Basin and Range Province. Under this ongoing regime of crustal thinning and stretching, the Basin and Range Province has continually foundered, all the while expanding its domain by listric calving of the retreating periphery of the Colorado Plateau. The current southwestern edge of the Colorado Plateau ramps down the Grand Wash Cliffs into the Grand Wash Trough, outermost of the many north-trending extensional basins that parade *en echelon* across the Mojave Desert from Arizona to California. Subsidence of this trough combined with concurrent uplift of the Colorado Plateau to generate 16,000 feet of vertical offset on the Grand Wash Fault at the mouth of the Grand Canyon by six million years ago.

Our modern west-flowing Colorado River (less than six million years old) has incised the Grand Canyon into the Colorado Plateau in its pursuit of hydraulic grade with the Grand Wash Trough. Where the Colorado River debouches onto the Basin and Range Province, the Grand Canyon loses its reason for being.

The desert, as though in tribute to the Grand Canyon for the water delivery, sends envoys of its own Mojave-Sonoran biota through the portal in the Grand Wash Cliffs into the very heart of the Colorado Plateau. The inverse variation of temperature with elevation spikes desert-temperature contours far up the Grand Canyon. The presence in the Inner Gorge and on the Esplanade of Lower Sonoran species such as Joshua trees, ocotillo, and honey mesquite—the latter as far upstream as Mile 40—exemplifies the *corridor effect* of temperature salients on biotic distribution.

The corridor effect might be expected to have invited the desert's human predators into the Grand Canyon at a time when the dying rigors of the Last Ice Age kept the top of the Colorado Plateau inhospitably cold. Within the Grand Canyon, the regional cooling associated with ice ages translates into downslope migration of temperature isograds. As a given temperature interval creeps downslope, so do the biota favored in that interval. Eleven thousand years ago, desert hunters rounding the first bend of the Grand Canyon would have found themselves surrounded by juniper trees rather than today's Joshua trees. How do we know?

Sloth dung. It so happens that Rampart Cave—640 feet above and half-a-mile larboard of River Mile 275; sunk into the foot of the Muav Limestone Grand Wash Cliffs—served as a convenience stop for Shasta ground sloths until just 11,000 years ago. Lamentably, only a fraction of the cave's dung deposits, copious when discovered in 1936, escaped carbonization by arsonists in 1976. Fortunately, identifiable plant fragments in datable dung had already enabled paleoecologists to reconstruct botanical successions in the vicinity of Rampart Cave.

Although ground sloths are extinct (some species as recently as a few hundred years ago), their living cousins, the tree sloths, provide clues to their extinguished functions. Ground sloths, like modern tree sloths, were strictly herbivorous. Too big to climb trees to get at foliage, ground sloths instead were able to jack themselves into a semibipedal stance to browse the upper branches of trees of choice. Juniper foliage was a Shasta favorite.

The plant material inside a modern sloth, steeping in its capacious multichambered stomach for a week before it is properly digested, constitutes a third of its body weight. Once a week, the sloth passes a very large batch of excrement. The Shasta ground sloth (*Northrotheriops shastense*) was only a quarter the size of another contemporary ground sloth (*Megatherium*) that was itself bigger than a modern elephant—but one-third the weight of a Shasta ground sloth was by no means trifling.

Its neighbors' toilet habits may help to explain the modern sloth's keen taste for solitude. Spending only ten per cent of its life in any kind of movement, one reclusive sloth will still occasionally blunder into another. Chance encounters erupt in T'ai Chi duels that are generally fatal to the slower sloth. Ground sloths were not only the first hermits of Grand Canyon but the smelliest and the orneriest.

Scientists have nevertheless taken a fancy to ground sloths for their unbuttoned testimony concerning bygone plant communities. Poring over the 30,000-year continuum of sloth dung from Rampart Cave, paleoecologists found, for example, that juniper trees grew abundantly in the area around Rampart Cave during the latest ice age and its aftermath. Rampart Cave's 1,800-foot elevation puts it squarely in the modern zone of desert scrub typified by cactus, whereas modern junipers do not occur below 4,500 feet. This 2,700-foot juniper discrepancy is interesting but hardly surprising. It seems perfectly reasonable, after all, that the Grand Canyon should have been a good deal colder during an ice age and wetter in its aftermath. Yet the dung archives did record a genuine surprise. The same barrel and hedgehog cacti that now grow in the area around Rampart Cave were growing there during the latest ice age (23,000 to 15,000 years ago), right alongside the juniper!

This cactus-juniper association, unknown today, suggests that seasonality less extreme than now obtains might have moderated the effects of ice-age frigidity on biota of the Grand Canyon. Summers must have been cool and moist enough to tolerate juniper trees at low elevation; winters must have been mild and dry enough to spare cacti.

Post-Pleistocene pluviation allowed junipers to persist in the Rampart Cave area despite secular warming until 8,400 years ago, when they began their steep upcountry retreat. By that date, however, no sloths remained atop their ramparts to adjure Birnam wood to halt. One is entitled to speculate that Desert Culture nomads had already penetrated the Canyon from the Mojave Desert and bagged the easy kill of Rampart Cave.

COLUMBINE FALLS, LOOKING SOUTH FROM MILE 275. These falls (also called Emery Falls) tumble down the lower Grand Wash Cliffs from springs in Muav Limestone. Limestone, although highly susceptible to acid erosion by water, proves a resistant cliff-former in the arid Grand Canyon region. Such water as does fall on the region mainly goes to ground, where it etches out subterranean channels for itself in limestone strata.

PHOTOGRAPH BY WILLARD CLAY

LEFT BANK OF THE COLORADO RIVER, MILE 275, BELOW RAMPART CAVE. The waterline shown in this photograph taken just inside the mouth of the Grand Canyon is that of Lake Mead. An artifact of Hoover Dam, completed in 1935 sixty miles downstream of the Grand Canyon, Lake Mead rises to a high-water mark of 1,221 feet above sea level. The backflooding of the western end of the Grand Canyon has increased the depth to riverbed at Mile 275 to 340 feet. The maximum depth of the free-flowing Colorado River within the Grand Canyon, by contrast, is only 100 feet.

The green of the water seen in the photograph is another anthropogenic novelty. Glen Canyon Dam, 16 miles upstream of the head of Grand Canyon, efficiently traps the sediment transported hundreds of miles by the Colorado River. The annual sediment load carried into the Grand Canyon, formerly as great as 500 million tons annually, has been negligible since the completion of Glen Canyon Dam in 1964. The dam's spillways tap clear water with a constant temperature of 48° F from 200 feet beneath the surface of 3,700-foot-deep Lake Powell. Moreover, dam regulation has severely damped the amplitude of the natural seasonal discharge cycle and imposed an artificial daily discharge cycle (locally referred to as the river's *tide*) indexed to metropolitan power demands that peak at midday.

Today, the Colorado River in the Grand Canyon is generally clear, cold, and cyclically steady. Prior to 1964, it was red ("too thick to drink; not thick enough to walk on"); warm (up to 86° F); and volumetrically erratic. *Colorado* (meaning *red* in Spanish) no longer describes the greenish river that flows through the Grand Canyon.

PHOTOGRAPH BY WILLARD CLAY

MOUNTAIN LION. Mountain lion scat is more often seen than the cat. The muscular mountain lion is so stealthy that hikers never suspect when they have been trailed for hours by the eight-foot-long (not counting the tail) predator. Commonly ranging 25 miles a night to set ambushes in ravines of plateau, woodland, and inner canyon, the mountain lion bulks up on mule deer at a rate of about one a week. It varies its viands with beaver, porcupine, and squirrel.

PHOTOGRAPH BY JEFF FOOTT

PHOTOGRAPH BY TOM TILL

ESPLANADE SEGMENT

THE ESPLANADE segment, embracing the western half of the Grand Canyon, is the longest and most neglected in the sequence of four segments into which the whole Grand Canyon is conveniently divided on the basis of side-canyon style. The Esplanade is the broad, topographically intermediate platform that typifies this segment. "Intermediate" with respect to what?

Let's work our way round to an answer to this question by shaking a few inductive rules out of the geological hurly-burly of the Grand Canyon.

1. *In the Grand Canyon region, the crust consists of a thick 1.7 billion-year-old metamorphic Precambrian basement together with its passive veneer of sedimentary strata.*

The thickness of the basement tapers from 25 miles under the Kaibab Plateau to 19 miles under the Grand Wash Cliffs, before decreasing abruptly to 15 miles on the basin-range side of the Grand Wash Fault. The overlying stack of sedimentary strata, predominantly Paleozoic in age, is about a mile thick.

2: *One especially tough Permian stratum—the 250 million-year-old Kaibab Limestone—roofs the sedimentary package almost everywhere in the Grand Canyon region.*

This rule obtains even though the originally continuous strata have been chopped up into discontinuous tracts by extensive north-trending fault-systems. Movement on these fault-systems of the Grand Canyon region has undergone a grand two-stroke cycle with a billion-year period.

The fault-systems of the Grand Canyon region initially developed in Precambrian times as west-facing normal faults to accommodate crustal stretching and thinning that ceased over 800 million years ago. Three-quarters of a billion years of inactivity on these faults ensued, by the end of which interval a two-mile thickness of Paleozoic and Mesozoic continental-shelf sediments had accumulated in neat strata above the horizontally stable erosion surface of the Precambrian basement.

At the close of the Mesozoic era some 70 million years ago, a violent new tectonic regime called the Laramide arose and appropriated the dormant faults for its own use. The ancient normal faults in the basement awakened to find themselves rejuvenated as reverse faults by east-west crustal shortening in response to the compressive stresses of the Laramide orogeny. Eastward thrusting on these west-facing faults propagated out of the Precambrian basement as east-verging asymmetrical flexures in the overlying sedimentary rock known as *monoclines*.

Extensional tectonism returned to the Grand Canyon region in the Miocene epoch 17 million years ago. The same Precambrian faults that had been exploited in the reverse sense by the Laramide compression were now reactivated in their original normal sense, severing and offsetting many of the monoclines in the sedimentary cover. Principal throughgoing normal faults in the Grand Canyon region define the modern boundaries of elevationally discrete blocks, idiomatically (and unsystematically) called *plateaux*.

Six named plateaux, each differentially downdropped along its eastern boundary, abut the Grand Canyon. Proceeding along the North Rim eastward from the Grand Wash Fault, the contiguous sequence is Shivwits Plateau (downdropped and tilted to the east on the Hurricane Fault, which crosses the Grand Canyon at Mile 191); Uinkaret Plateau (downdropped and tilted to the east on the Toroweap Fault, Mile 179); Kanab Plateau (downdropped and tilted to the east on the West Kaibab Fault Zone, Mile 99); and Kaibab Plateau (upwarped into a dome that scrolls eastward over the essentially intact East Kaibab Monocline onto the low-lying Marble Platform, Mile 65). The continuation of the Shivwits Plateau southward of the Grand Canyon is called the Hualapai Plateau; the southward continuations of the Uinkaret, Kanab, and Kaibab Plateaux are amalgamated under the rubric of Coconino Plateau. This mosaic of six lesser plateaux and one platform is said to constitute the southwestern corner of the higher-order Colorado *Plateau*. Finally, to sock in the toponymic fog, the lesser plateaux can spin off their own little satellite plateaux: Kaibab Plateau has its outlier Walhalla *Plateau*; Kanab Plateau has its outlier Powell *Plateau*.

We can now refine our second rule in accordance with the customary physiographic description: *Kaibab Limestone caps the stratigraphy of all of the plateaux in the Grand Canyon region, except one.* The exception, the Hualapai Plateau, is capped by older (Carboniferous) Redwall Limestone. The big north-trending Hurricane, Toroweap, and East Kaibab Monoclines of the Laramide stepped the Paleozoic strata down toward the east. As well, the strata dipped regionally to the northeast. The erosion surface that planed across the Grand Canyon region in the Laramide, as a result, exposed oldest strata in the southwest. That is why only the southwesternmost of the Grand Canyon's modern plateaux is totally denuded of the Kaibab Limestone stratum.

The geometric interplay between underlying structure and surficial erosion governs the ages of rocks exposed. As just noted, progressively older rocks are exposed westward in the western Grand Canyon (for example, the Precambrian rocks of the Lower Granite Gorge between Miles 261 and 216) by the Laramide interplay between monoclinal vergence and erosional planation. On a shorter scale, progressively older rocks are exposed westward within each individual plateau of the western Grand Canyon by the sympathetic interplay of Miocene block-tilting down to the east and post-Miocene erosional incision of the Grand Canyon (also exemplified by the Lower Granite Gorge). Older rocks are exposed in the eastern Grand Canyon by the interplay between Laramide upwarping of the Kaibab dome and post-Miocene incision by the modern Colorado River (for example, the Precambrian rocks of the Upper Granite Gorge, between Miles 118 and 77).

TRAVERTINE CANYON (LEFT BANK, MILE 224).
PHOTOGRAPH BY FRED HIRSCHMANN

LIMESTONE, KELLY POINT, SHIVWITS PLATEAU. This limestone, a skeletal packstone containing a high proportion of disarticulated crinoid (sea-lily) columnals in a micritic matrix, represents a carbonate lithofacies of the Brady Canyon Member of the Permian Toroweap Formation. The Brady Canyon Member and the Toroweap Formation as a whole both exemplify the general trends in the Paleozoic strata of the Grand Canyon region of eastward thinning and eastward attenuation of carbonate content.

    The open-marine fauna that typifies the Brady Canyon member in the western Grand Canyon region yields eastward to a restricted-marine fauna. The member also thins eastward, to a depositional feather-edge just west of Marble Canyon. The Toroweap Formation as a whole thins eastward from 330 feet thickness at Kelly Point, where it is mostly carbonate, to 180 feet at Marble Canyon, where it is exclusively sandstone.

PHOTOGRAPH BY JACK W. DYKINGA

3. *Paleozoic strata thicken westward in the Grand Canyon region.*

Throughout the Paleozoic era, the Grand Canyon region sat on the western continental shelf of North American. Over this span of a third of a billion years, the shoreline raced to (during eastward marine transgression) and fro (during westward marine regression) across the shelf hundreds of times in response to competing rates of change in global eustasy, plate tectonism, and local subsidence. Whether submerged or emergent, the top of the sedimentary pile was never more than a few hundred feet from sea level.

Although the Grand Canyon region spent only about a third of the Paleozoic era underwater, most of the surviving Paleozoic rocks are limestones, shales, and sandstones composed of various marine sediments. This representational disproportion arose because submerged sites receive more sediments and are more likely to be preserved than emergent sites.

Intervals of emergence at a given site on the Paleozoic continental shelf are typically represented by gaps in the rock record. Bypassed by sediment transport systems seeking lowlying depocenters offshore to the west, emergent land tended to be starved of new incoming sediment. Worse, subaerial erosion continually cut into the crumbling inheritance of old sediment. An impressive instance of such a gap, or *unconformity*, in the Paleozoic stratigraphy of the Grand Canyon region is the Cambrian-Early Mississippian Unconformity. This dimensionless horizon between the Redwall and Muav Limestones sucked 180 million years of regional history into oblivion.

The bourne of the terrestrial sediment clattering down the rivers across the Paleozoic continental shelf was the muffled seafloor. Crustal thickening at offshore depocenters was isostatically adjusted by subsidence of the marine sedimentary pile. Since the subsiding shelf rotated rigidly about a landward hinge, progressively greater thicknesses of marine sediments were accommodated in the seaward direction.

During the Paleozoic era, then, differential rates of subsidence increased westward. Moreover, during each marine transgression, the Grand Canyon region was underwater earlier and longer in the west than in the east. Consequently, with respect to each transgressive episode, sediments were older and rates of sedimentation were higher in the west. Conversely, with respect to each regressive episode, erosion began earlier in the east. These paleogeographic considerations explain why Paleozoic strata in the Grand Canyon region attenuate eastward in both thickness and carbonate content. For example, the thickness of the Muav Limestone stratum, as it youngs to the east, dwindles from a robust 827 feet in the Grand Wash Cliffs at Mile 277 to only 136 feet in Buck Farm Canyon at Mile 41.

LICHEN, KANAB POINT (5,779 FEET).
PHOTOGRAPH BY TOM TILL

The westward thickening of Paleozoic strata explains a puzzle. The 1,330-foot decrease in elevation of the Colorado River from Miles 77 to 237 is roughly commensurate with the 1,500-foot decrease in elevation of the Kaibab Limestone stratum as projected over the same River Miles. Given the Laramide beveling of the strata in the southwestern Grand Canyon region, one would expect the Lower Granite Gorge of the western Grand Canyon to bite more deeply into the Precambrian basement than the Upper Granite Gorge of the eastern Grand Canyon. Westward thickening of Paleozoic strata by several thousand feet explains why, in fact, the Upper Granite Gorge bites into Precambrian basement more deeply than the Lower Granite Gorge.

4. *Topographically intermediate platforms within the Grand Canyon form upon a resistant stratum that is overlain by a readily erodible stratum.*

The westward thickening of Paleozoic strata also explains why the intermediate topography of the western Grand Canyon is dominated by a platform of Esplanade Sandstone, whereas the eastern Grand Canyon is dominated by the stratigraphically lower Tonto Platform.

The Tonto Platform has formed on the Cambrian resistant/erodible couplet of Tapeats Sandstone/Bright Angel Shale. Erosion of Bright Angel Shale undermines overlying resistant Muav Limestone. Muav Limestone, it will be recalled, is quite thin here. Having lost its much thicker Bright Angel Shale foundation, it spalls off readily. The cap of Muav Limestone does not effectively retard the erosional retreat of Bright Angel Shale.

The cap of Muav Limestone in the western Grand Canyon, where it is six times thicker, does effectively retard the retreat of Bright Angel Shale. The Bright Angel bench is a weenie. The dominant platform here has formed on the Permian resistant/erodible couplet of Esplanade Sandstone/Hermit Shale. The Hermit Shale Formation is 900 feet thick in the west, against only 100 feet in the east. The overlying Coconino Sandstone, on the other hand, is only 60 feet thick in both the east and the west. This exception to the westward-thickening rule is accounted for by the terrestrial origin of the Coconino Sandstone, which is made of lithified sand dunes of a Permian *erg* desert as vast as the modern Sahara. The thin cap of Coconino Sandstone does not effectively retard the erosional retreat of the Hermit Shale.

To return to the innocent question that prompted this geological disquisition: The Esplanade is a prominent bench in the western half of the Grand Canyon that is topographically intermediate between an inner gorge bottoming in either Cambrian or Precambrian rocks and a rim which is Late Permian Kaibab Limestone everywhere but on the Hualapai Plateau, where it is the older (Late Mississippian) Redwall Limestone.

Most side canyons of the Esplanade segment, such as the Toroweap Valley separating the Uinkaret and Kanab Plateaux, trace sections of the set of north-trending faults that demarcate the Shivwits, Uinkaret, Hualapai, and western Kanab and Coconino Plateaux. Accordingly, they are long and linear, as well as broad at the level of the Esplanade. The course of the Colorado River itself is controlled by the north-trending Hurricane Fault Zone between Miles 214 and 227. Numerous fossil canyons in the Esplanade segment—as well as a few active side canyons, such as that of Havasu Creek—preserve the old regional northwest trend followed by the ancestral upper Colorado River after its turn on the Kaibab Dome.

VIEW FROM THE SUMMIT OF MOUNT DELLENBAUGH, SHIVWITS PLATEAU, LOOKING SUCCESSIVELY PAST GREEN SPRING CANYON AND SPRING CANYON (MILE 194) TO AUBREY CLIFFS ON THE SKYLINE (APRIL). The 7,072-foot high summit of Mount Dellenbaugh is composed, like most of the cap of the Shivwits Plateau, of upper Miocene basalt lava flows extruded 7.5 to 6.0 million years ago. Many of the basalt flows on the Uinkaret Plateau bear peridotite xenoliths ripped from the upper mantle at a depth of about fifty miles. In the side canyons of the Colorado River that invade the perimeter of the Shivwits Plateau, such as Green Spring Canyon, no trace of these voluminous plateau basalts is to be found. The implication is that the western Grand Canyon was incised more recently than six million years ago. Hurricane Fault, the eastern boundary of the Shivwits/Hualapai Plateaux, runs between and parallel to the Colorado River and Aubrey Cliffs. The stretch between Miles 214 and 227 represents the only part of the course of the Colorado River in the Grand Canyon that is fault-controlled.

PHOTOGRAPH BY JACK W. DYKINGA

TOROWEAP VALLEY, LOOKING FROM ONE MILE NORTH OF TOROWEAP OVERLOOK (ABOVE RIGHT BANK, MILE 177) NORTH TO TOROWEAP POINT. We are standing on the Esplanade in front of grizzly bear cactus (*Opuntia erinacea*), Colorado four o'clock (*Mirabilis multiflora*), and century plant (*Agave utahensis*). The face of Toroweap Point rises up from the Esplanade Sandstone platform through Hermit Shale and Coconino Sandstone to the Toroweap Formation. The view in this photograph duplicates a fraction of one of William Holmes' astonishingly lucid panoramic drawings (namely, Sheet V) in Clarence Dutton's *Tertiary History of the Grand Cañon District* (1882).

Toroweap (also called *Tuweep*) Valley, controlled by the master Toroweap Fault separating the Uinkaret and Kanab Plateaux, is long and linear to the north and broad at the level of the Esplanade. This side-canyon morphology is characteristic of the Esplanade segment.

PHOTOGRAPH BY FRED HIRSCHMANN

GRIZZLY BEAR CACTUS (MILE 108).   This common cactus blooms pink in May-June.

PHOTOGRAPH BY LARRY ULRICH

COLORADO FOUR O'CLOCK (*Mirabilis multiflora*).
PHOTOGRAPH BY LARRY ULRICH

CLARET CUP CACTUS AND FALLEN CENTURY PLANT, KELLY POINT, SHIVWITS PLATEAU (APRIL). This common cactus (*Echinocereus triglochidiatus*) blooms red each April-June. The century plant (*Agave utahensis*), after 15-25 uneventful years, shoots out a stalk up to 14 feet high on which yellow flowers bloom for just one summer. Exhausted by this singular reproductive thrust, the plant dies.

PHOTOGRAPH BY JACK W. DYKINGA

CENTURY PLANT WITH COLORADO PINYON PINE-CONE, KELLY POINT, SHIVWITS PLATEAU. The dagger-like leaves of the century plant (*Agave utahensis)* are distinguished from those of the yucca family by the curved thorns serrating the margins of the former. The century plant in the Grand Canyon region ranges from river to rim, overlapping the Upper Sonoran range of the pinyon pine (*Pinus edulis*). The Indians of Grand Canyon ate both roasted agave shoots and pinyon pine-seeds.

PHOTOGRAPH BY JACK W. DYKINGA

VIEW WESTWARD FROM TOROWEAP OVERLOOK (SUNSET). Remnants of the Toroweap Lava Dam are visible high on the canyon walls of the left bank.

PHOTOGRAPH BY LARRY ULRICH

VIEW EASTWARD FROM TOROWEAP OVERLOOK (SUNRISE). The iron-oxide-stained rock on which we are standing is sandstone of the Esplanade Sandstone Formation, which is 400 feet thick in the Toroweap Valley. The dozens of climbing, cross-stratified sets making up this formation indicate that the Esplanade Sandstone is composed of lithified dunes.

PHOTOGRAPH BY DAVID MUENCH

CASCADES OF NAVAJO FALLS, HAVASU CANYON (MARCH). These travertine falls are not named for the Navajo Indians, who had nothing to do with Havasu Canyon. They commemorate rather an Havasupai chief of the latter part of the nineteenth century. Chief Navajo served as a scout for the U.S. Army in its campaign in central Arizona against the Yavapai Indians — hated relatives of the Havasupai and Hualapai tribes. Later, Chief Navajo led his people in observance of the Second Ghost Dance, promulgated by Wovoka. Wovoka, a Northern Paiute from western Arizona who had syncretized Presbyterian and Mormon elements with traditional shaman-prophecy, gouged stigmata into his hands and feet in order to portray himself as Jesus Christ, come to the Indians to deliver their besieged culture.

PHOTOGRAPH BY JEFF GNASS

Havasu Creek is the biggest tributary in the Grand Canyon after the Little Colorado River. Yet Colorado River voyageurs rounding Mile 157 must look hard a-port to spot the discreet alley in Muav Limestone through which warm Havasu Creek disgorges into the cold, swift-flowing river.

The view up Havasu Canyon from its mouth is limited to a few hundred yards by its narrowness and tortuosity. By contrast, the view that we shall see up Bright Angel Canyon from Mile 88 is unimpeded for ten miles. Fault-controlled Bright Angel Canyon is broad and linear; fold-controlled Havasu Canyon is narrow and curvilinear.

Below Supai Village, a ten-mile tramp up Havasu Creek from its confluence with the Colorado River, Havasu Canyon is bounded on the east by the northwest-striking Supai Monocline. This monocline steps down to the west, oppositely to the sense of most monoclines of the Grand Canyon region. Above Supai Village, Havasu Canyon traces the axis of the northwest-plunging Havasu Downwarp, an extension of Cataract Basin to the southeast. The Havasu/Cataract structural sag offsets the structural swell of the Kaibab upwarp to the east. Sag and swell were imposed as complementary elements of a regional wave-form by Laramide east-west compression.

This structural sag has enabled the eighty-mile-long Havasu/Cataract Creek to preserve adventitiously the old northwesterly trend that dominated drainage in the Grand Canyon region for scores of millions of years. This dominion ended in the Pliocene, when, as we have seen, regional dip-control relaxed at the same time that the modern Colorado River began slashing west across the country. Confinement of Havasu Creek to the trough of an unbroken flexure in the strata (as opposed to the laterally extensive erosion that characterizes a pervasively broken fault-zone, as in Bright Angel Canyon) has given Havasu Canyon walls that are not only serpentine but forbiddingly steep.

The natives of Havasu Canyon, the Havasupai, traditionally negotiated the precipitous walls of their canyon home by means of fragile wooden ladders. The Havasupai are descendants of Yuman-speaking Cerbat Indians of the lower Colorado River basin who moved into Havasu Canyon in the mid-twelfth century, replacing the former Cohonina tenants. The Havasupai are broad-faced, light-framed, and nimble.

SCARLET MONKEY-FLOWERS AND BOX-ELDER, HAVASU CREEK. The scarlet (also called *crimson* or *cardinal*) monkey-flower (*Mimulus cardinalis*) is a member of the Snapdragon Family that thrives in the shade beside seeps and streams. It blooms March-October. Box-elder (*Acer negundo*), a member of the Maple Family, prefers moist but sunny areas.

PHOTOGRAPH BY LARRY ULRICH

Summers are diabolically hot and dry in Havasu Canyon. In July, the average daily high is 106 degrees F and there is less than an inch of rainfall. The close bare rock walls of the canyon baffle the reflective component of the high-angle summer insolation. Heat irradiating from the walls maintains very low relative humidity in the air over Havasu Creek. Under such conditions, the exsolution and evaporation rates from Havasu Creek are high. The partial pressure of carbon dioxide in the creek goes down; the concentration of calcium carbonate solute goes up. Calcium carbonate is obliged to precipitate. Precipitation initiates at numberless dispersed submicroscopic sites in the creekwater, turning it milky.

The suspended particles of calcium carbonate tend to encrust the surface of any object over which Havasu Creek flows. Encrustation is favored by greater area of substrate and slower stream velocity. As a corollary, travertine deposition, once begun, is self-enhancing. Encrustation enlarges the substrate area and further impedes stream-flow, leading to more encrustation, and so on. Conversely, the spillways across these dams are preserved by self-restriction of travertine deposition. As a spillway constricts by lateral growth of the dam, increased stream velocity in the spillway inhibits accretion of calcium carbonate particles. Self-enhancement has cooperated with self-restriction to give Havasu Creek its fanciful flights of flat-topped, sinuous travertine dams pierced by spouts of gushing water.

Marching down the defile of Havasu Canyon are three orderly columns of green, blue, and green abreast. The creek, a bone-powdered blue, imbues its banks with the saturated-green lushness of a quirky association of plants: cottonwoods, willows, velvet ash, monkey-flowers, wild grape, ferns, mosses, prickly-pear cacti. Even the human residents are color-coordinated with their ribbon of paradise: *Havasu/pai* means "blue-green/people."

Yet every earthly paradise is surely cankered. The lines of gnarled cottonwoods that dip their thirsty roots into perennial tributaries such as Havasu Creek (though not the Colorado River itself) appear at first more sinned against than sinning. Cottonwood bark toothe beaver's palate is to die for. One beaver will fell a five-inch-diameter cottonwood in three minutes to glut itself on the toothsome cortex. Gluttony can harm more than a beaver's moral symmetry, however, for the loose bark of the cottonwood harbors an exceedingly nasty arachnid. Up to three inches long, the bark (or *slender*) scorpion (*Centruroides sculpturatus*) packs venom more neurotoxic than a rattler's and killing four times more people each year in Arizona. The pain of its sting is followed by local numbness; then a spreading tingliness; then tightening of the throat; then drooling; then blindness; finally, frothing convulsions. In Mexico, Centruroides kill 160 people a year.

This pale solitary killer yields on rare occasion to an impulse to intimacy and stalks the night for a rumba partner. Once the mincing *promenade à deux* to the castanet-click of the male's slender pedipalps is consummated, woe to the male scorpion who lets down his trichobothria and tarries to savor the tender moment! One last savage kiss by his unrequiting inamorata, and the male's soft parts are slurped out.

Others prefer the hard parts. Serious collectors equip themselves with black light: scorpions' chitinous cuticles, except when still soft after any of five moltings, fluoresce beautifully in UV.

VIEW FROM KANAB POINT, LOOKING SOUTHWEST ALONG NORTH RIM; OVER INNER CANYON; TO MOUNT SINYALA AND COCONINO PLATEAU ON SKYLINE (APRIL, MORNING).

PHOTOGRAPH BY TOM TILL

MATKATAMIBA CANYON (LEFT BANK, MILE 148). Matkatamiba Canyon is controlled by the Matkatamiba Syncline, a concave-upward fold parallel to and associated with the Supai Monocline/Havasupai Downwarp system that controls Havasu Canyon. The steep, narrow, tortuous Muav Limestone walls shown in this photograph resemble on a smaller scale those of Havasu Canyon. The common morphology of Matkatamiba and Havasu Canyons is determined by the unbroken character of the controlling flexures in the rock.

PHOTOGRAPH BY TOM TILL

KAIBAB SEGMENT

T HE KAIBAB morphological segment of the Grand Canyon extends from Kanab Creek at Mile 143 to the eastern end of the Upper Granite Gorge at Mile 77. Along most of this sixty-six-river-mile stretch, the Colorado River is channeled by the steep walls, hewn in Precambrian basement rock, of the Inner Granite Gorge. The Granite Gorge of this segment is parsed into two sections: Granite Narrows and the Middle Granite Gorge between Miles 137 and 127; and the Upper Granite Gorge between Miles 118 and 77. As we have seen, incision by the Colorado River has exposed such a generous swath of Precambrian rock along this stretch because it cores the Kaibab Dome and because the overlying Paleozoic strata are relatively thin in the eastern Grand Canyon.

The radial geometry of the Kaibab Dome dictates the organization of drainage on the North Rim of the Kaibab segment. Fed by subterranean meltwater from the several feet of snow that fall each winter on the Kaibab Plateau, perennial streams—such as Deer Creek, Thunder River, and Bright Angel Creek—radiate down the western and southern flanks of the Kaibab Dome. Their canyons, localized by fault zones, are typically long, broad, and elaborately dendritic. The whittled landforms separating these radial side canyons of the North Rim constitute the phantasmagoria of temples and thrones, pyres and pyramids, cloisters and castles that has conferred star status on the Kaibab segment.

The organization of drainage on the South Rim of the Kaibab segment, on the other hand, is dictated by the antagonism between the slope of the Grand Canyon (north and east) and the dip of the strata (south and west). Because aquifers in Coconino Plateau flow away from the Grand Canyon and comparatively little precipitation falls there in the first place (16 inches of precipitation annually, versus 27 inches on the Kaibab Plateau), South Rim tributaries of the Colorado River in the Kaibab segment are short and ephemeral. Their canyons, in contrast to the side canyons on the other side of the river, are short, narrow, and unbranched.

GRANITE NARROWS, LOOKING FROM RIGHT BANK, MILE 136. The rocks exposed in the Granite Narrows are Vishnu Schist, 1.7 billion years old. The dodecahedral crystals of almandine garnet studding the rocks in this mile-long corridor reveal that the pressures of formation here were the highest to have affected the Vishnu Metamorphic Complex. High grade of metamorphism determines high resistance to erosion. Granite Narrows is therefore very steep and narrow. Here, the Colorado River constricts to its least width (76 feet) in the Grand Canyon.

Although *Narrows* is apt, *Granite* is another of Powell's unhappy misnomers. Granite is an isotropic igneous rock; schist is a foliated metamorphic rock. This nomenclatural distinction was well-established by the beginning of the nineteenth century and was properly applied by Dutton, Powell's colleague, to the basement rocks exposed in the Inner Gorge.

PHOTOGRAPH BY LARRY ULRICH

TAPEATS SANDSTONE, DEER CREEK CANYON (RIGHT BANK, MILE 136) (JULY).

PHOTOGRAPH BY TOM TILL

HAND PICTOGRAPHS, DEER CREEK CANYON.
PHOTOGRAPH BY FRED HIRSCHMANN

UPPER DEER CREEK FALLS (RIGHT BANK, MILE 136).
PHOTOGRAPH BY DAVID MUENCH

TRAVERTINE DOME, STONE CREEK
CANYON (RIGHT BANK, MILE 132).
PHOTOGRAPH BY FRED HIRSCHMANN

THUNDER SPRINGS, TAPEATS CREEK CANYON (SEPTEMBER,
MORNING). Thunder Springs is the headwater of Thunder River, a
perennial tributary of Tapeats Creek, itself a tributary of the Colorado
River on the right bank at Mile 134. Thunder Springs bursts out of
Muav Limestone, under hydraulic head from the Kanab Plateau melt-
water percolating across the overlying Redwall Limestone.

PHOTOGRAPH BY TOM TILL

COLORADO RIVER, LOOKING DOWNSTREAM FROM MOUTH OF
STONE CREEK CANYON (RIGHT BANK, MILE 132).

PHOTOGRAPH BY LARRY ULRICH

CRIMSON MONKEY-FLOWER IN ELVES
CHASM, ROYAL ARCH CREEK (LEFT
BANK, MILE 116).

PHOTOGRAPH BY LARRY ULRICH

VIEW FROM POINT SUBLIME, LOOKING WEST PAST SAGITTARIUS RIDGE TO MOUNT HUETHAWALI (CENTER BACKGROUND), POWELL PLATEAU (RIGHT SKYLINE), AND THE UINKARET MOUNTAINS (SKY-LINE). On the skyline, two peaks in the Uinkaret Mountains are conspicuous: Mount Trumbull (8,028 feet) and Mount Emma (7,698 feet). These "mounts" are actually mounds: basaltic cones formed about 1.5 million years ago in alignment west of and parallel to the Toroweap Fault, the west-facing, high-angle normal fault that splits the Toroweap Valley and divides the Uinkaret from the Kanab Plateau. The younger age and greater relief of the Uinkaret Mountains capping the Uinkaret Plateau compared to the lavas capping the Shivwits Plateau demonstrate that the locus of vulcanism shifted eastward. This eastward migration of the volcanic fields symptomizes the continuing expansion of the Basin and Range extensional tectonic province at the expense of the Colorado Plateau.

The West Kaibab Fault Zone, separating Kanab Plateau from the Kaibab Plateau on which we are standing, runs east of and parallel to Hermit Shale-capped Sagittarius Ridge in the middle ground.

This view in this photograph duplicates a fraction of one of William Holmes' masterly panoramic drawings (namely, Sheet XVII) in Clarence Dutton's *Tertiary History of the Grand Cañon District* (1882).

PHOTOGRAPH BY DAVID MUENCH

VIEW NORTHEAST FROM THE SOUTH RIM OVER THE ABYSS, THE
MOJAVE WALL, AND THE ALLIGATOR TO ISIS TEMPLE (RIGHT)
AND TOWER OF SET (LEFT), NORTH RIM.

PHOTOGRAPH BY LARRY ULRICH

ISIS TEMPLE (LEFT) AND CHEOPS
PYRAMID (RIGHT), LOOKING NORTH
THROUGH LIMESTONE WINDOW,
SOUTH RIM. Isis Temple (7,012 feet) is
capped with Permian Coconino Sandstone;
Cheops Pyramid (5,392 feet), with Mississip-
pian Redwall Limestone.

PHOTOGRAPH BY DAVID MUENCH

VIEW NORTH FROM MOJAVE POINT TO TOWER OF SET (CLEARING WINTER STORM).

PHOTOGRAPH BY WILLARD CLAY

VIEW NORTHEAST FROM MOJAVE POINT (SOUTH RIM) OVER DANA BUTTE TO NINETYONE MILE CREEK (RIGHT BANK) (MAY, SUNSET).

PHOTOGRAPH BY JEFF GNASS

VISHNU SCHIST, GRANITE GORGE. Rocks of the Vishnu Metamorphic Complex are exposed in the Lower (Miles 261-216), Middle (137-127), and Upper (118-77) Granite Gorges. These rocks originated two billion years ago as sands, muds, and lavas laid upon an island-arc seafloor on the margin of the North American craton. An intense compressive episode here 1.7 billion years ago cooked the rocks at 700 degrees and imparted to them the near-vertical, northwest-striking schistose foliation seen here.

PHOTOGRAPH BY LARRY ULRICH

GRANITE RAPIDS, LOOKING UPSTREAM TO DANA BUTTE FROM THE MONUMENT CREEK DEBRIS FAN PROJECTING FROM THE LEFT BANK, MILE 93.

PHOTOGRAPH BY TOM TILL

GRANITE RAPIDS, LOOKING UPSTREAM TO DANA BUTTE FROM THE MONUMENT CREEK DEBRIS FAN PROJECTING FROM THE LEFT BANK, MILE 93 (SUNSET). The surface of the Colorado River drops 17 feet in a quarter of a mile across Granite Rapids. By contrast, the drop across the half-mile stretch of the river above Granite Rapids is imperceptible. This coupling of a fairly flat, tranquil liquid tread with a steep, turbulent foaming riser is repeated 160 times along the course of the Colorado River through the Grand Canyon. These 160 rapids account for only a tenth of the length of the river from Lees Ferry to Lake Mead but fully half of the 1,886-foot drop in river-level. This staircase on the water surface does not mimic a staircase in the riverbed. The watery staircase is an hydraulic effect of constriction at the rapids. Virtually all the rapids in the Grand Canyon occur where the Colorado River is constricted by debris fans at the mouths of tributaries. Because they are much steeper, tributaries are competent to deliver to the riverbed individual boulders and aggregate debris flows too large for natural floods of the Colorado River (much less the post-Glen Canyon Dam discharge maxima) to clear readily. The debris fan of Monument Creek on which we are standing in the photograph, for example, was augmented in 1984 by a debris flow a tenth of a cubic mile in volume. This debris flow, triggered by slope failure after heavy rain, took only two minutes to deliver boulders nine feet in diameter to the fan.

The rock of the Inner Gorge visible in this photograph is all Vishnu Schist except for the prominent light-colored band cutting the cliffs. This straight band is a highly differentiated igneous sill composed of Trinity Gneiss, intruded into the schist late in the Mazatzal compressive episode, 1.7 billion years ago.

Dana Butte, 2,680 feet above us on the skyline, is composed of vertical-walled Mississippian Redwall Limestone over Cambrian Muav Limestone. The saddle connecting the knob of Redwall Limestone at the end of the butte is a lens of Devonian Temple Butte Limestone.

PHOTOGRAPH BY TOM TILL

VIEW ACROSS BRIGHT ANGEL CANYON TO DEVA, BRAHMA, AND ZOROASTER TEMPLES (CENTER-LEFT) AND WOTAN'S THRONE AND VISHNU TEMPLE (CENTER), LOOKING NORTHEAST FROM HOPI WALL ON SOUTH RIM PAST HOPI POINT (WINTER). On the South Rim, Hopi Point (7,065 feet; capped with Permian Kaibab Limestone) is topographically joined to Dana Butte (5,030 feet; capped with Mississippian Redwall Limestone) by a mile-and-a-half-long ridge separating two side canyons (those of Salt and Horn Creeks) that are short (two miles long), simple, narrow, and steep.

On the North Rim, by contrast, Obi Point (7,928 feet; capped with Kaibab Limestone) is topographically joined

to the five-mile-long succession of Deva, Brahma, and Zoroaster Temples (capped with Permian Toroweap Formation). This row of "temples" constitutes a ridge between two side canyons (those of Bright Angel and Clear Creeks) that are long (15 miles long in the case of Bright Angel Canyon), dendritic, broad, and straight. The second-order side canyons that cut the ridge into "temples" are, like the first-order side canyons, fault-controlled.

In the Kaibab segment, the North Rim's side canyons are long, broad, and dendritic; whereas the South Rim's are short, narrow, and simple. This contrast reflects the North Rim's sympathetic stratal dip and greater precipitation, both owing to the position of the North Rim high on the southern flank of the Kaibab Dome.

PHOTOGRAPH BY KATHLEEN NORRIS COOK

VIEW ACROSS BRIGHT ANGEL CANYON TO
DEVA AND BRAHMA TEMPLES, LOOKING
NORTHEAST FROM HOPI POINT (STORM).
PHOTOGRAPH BY DAVID MUENCH

UPPER RIBBON FALLS, BRIGHT ANGEL CANYON.
We are standing on Precambrian Unkar Group rocks
deposited 1.2 billion years ago: Hakatai Shale under cliff-
forming Shinumo Quartzite.
PHOTOGRAPH BY DAVID MUENCH

DEAD JUNIPER AND BLACKBRUSH SCRUB,
TONTO PLATFORM. Blackbrush is a Rose Family shrub that has tangled, spiny branches and, from
March to May, small yellow flowers. Favored by
shaly soil, blackbrush grows abundantly, often in
pure stands, on the Bright Angel Shale surface of
the Tonto Platform. Blackbrush does not grow on
the Marble Platform, even though its elevation is
comparable to the 4,000-foot elevation of the
Tonto Platform. The Kaibab Limestone substrate
of the Marble Platform favors saltbush instead.
Juniper trees can extend their usual Upper Sonoran
lower range of 4,500 feet down onto the Tonto
Platform along ephemeral watercourses.
PHOTOGRAPH BY JAMES RANDKLEV

VIEW PAST MAPLES DOWN BRIGHT
ANGEL CANYON FROM NORTH KAIBAB
TRAIL (OCTOBER).
    PHOTOGRAPH BY RANDY A. PRENTICE

ROARING SPRINGS, BRIGHT ANGEL
CANYON. Roaring Springs are the perennial source of Bright Angel Creek. Meltwater from the Kaibab Plateau, having
percolated downdip through the permeable
limestone strata, bounds out at the base of
the Muav Limestone and spills over the
slope of Bright Angel Shale, as depicted in
the photograph.
    PHOTOGRAPH BY DAVID MUENCH

VIEW FROM BRIGHT ANGEL POINT ON THE NORTH RIM, LOOKING SOUTH DOWN BRIGHT ANGEL CANYON PAST THE SUCCESSION OF DEVA, BRAHMA, AND ZOROASTER TEMPLES TO THE COCONINO PLATEAU AND THE SAN FRANCISCO PEAKS ON THE SKYLINE (DECEMBER, SUNSET). The San Francisco Peaks, named by seventeenth-century priests of the Oraibi mission for the founder of their order, include the highest point in Arizona. Located near the southern margin of the Coconino Plateau sixty miles to the southeast of Bright Angel Point, the San Francisco Peaks are erosional remnants of the rim of a composite basaltic volcano that grew in five eruptive stages beginning 2.78 million years ago.

PHOTOGRAPH BY TOM TILL

ZOROASTER TEMPLE, LOOKING EAST
FROM VICINITY OF NORTH KAIBAB TRAIL.
PHOTOGRAPH BY MARC MUENCH

BRAHMA TEMPLE, LOOKING NORTHWEST FROM SOUTH RIM.
Toroweap Formation (ledges) caps Brahma Temple (7,551 feet). In descending order, the other strata composing Brahma Temple are Coconino Sandstone (cliff); Hermit Shale (slope); Esplanade Sandstone (cliff); and Lower Supai Group (ledges).

PHOTOGRAPH BY MARC MUENCH

BRAHMA (LEFT) AND ZOROASTER (RIGHT) TEMPLES, LOOKING SOUTHEAST FROM WIDFORSS POINT, NORTH RIM (SUNSET).
PHOTOGRAPH BY DAVID MUENCH

VIEW PAST O'NEILL BUTTE (SOUTH RIM) TO WOTAN'S THRONE (NORTH RIM), LOOKING NORTHEAST FROM YAVAPAI POINT (JULY, STORM). Sharing the view with a juniper tree on Kaibab Limestone at 7,040 feet, we are looking down upon O'Neill Butte (6,071 feet), capped with a spot of Hermit Shale atop Esplanade Sandstone cliffs that rise above Lower Supai Group ledges. Rainbows abound in Grand Canyon's *virga* (rain that evaporates before hitting the ground).

PHOTOGRAPH BY RANDY A. PRENTICE

VIEW PAST PINYON PINE AND YAKI POINT (SOUTH RIM) TO VISHNU TEMPLE, NORTHEAST FROM MATHER POINT (APRIL, SUNRISE).

PHOTOGRAPH BY TOM TILL

VIEW PAST YAKI POINT (SOUTH RIM) TO VISHNU TEMPLE, WOTAN'S THRONE, AND WALHALLA PLATEAU (NORTH RIM), LOOKING NORTHEAST FROM MATHER POINT (AFTERNOON).

PHOTOGRAPH BY LARRY ULRICH

VIEW PAST YAKI POINT AND O'NEILL BUTTE (SOUTH RIM) TO VISHNU TEMPLE
AND WOTAN'S THRONE (NORTH RIM), LOOKING NORTHEAST FROM MATHER
POINT (SNOWY, SUNRISE). A plaque at Mather Point (7,118 feet) honors Stephen T. Mather,
the borax magnate from Chicago who in 1917 became the first director of the National Park Ser-
vice and spent his private fortune on the infrastructure of the public parks.

PHOTOGRAPH BY CARR CLIFTON

"DUCK-ON-A-ROCK" HOODOO, SOUTH RIM, LOOKING EAST TO VISHNU TEMPLE AND RISING SUN. Hoodoos are pinnacles that emerge as erosional features in horizontal strata of heterogeneous hardness in arid climates. The host stratum of the hoodoos on the Grand Canyon rims is the Fossil Mountain Member of the Kaibab Limestone Formation. In the eastern Grand Canyon, this Member is somewhat thinner (250 feet thick) and much sandier and more dolomitized (magnesium-enriched) than it is in the western Grand Canyon. Hardness in the Member varies laterally as a function of biogenic (mainly sponge spicule) chert concentration and of spatial patterns of dolomitization, reflecting ancient migration paths of hypersaline fluids during diagenetic alteration of the limestone.

PHOTOGRAPH BY DAVID MUENCH

WOTAN'S THRONE, LOOKING SOUTHWEST FROM BELOW CAPE ROYAL, NORTH RIM (SEPTEMBER, SUNSET). Wotan's Throne (7,721 feet) is a Kaibab Limestone-capped mesa, a third of a square mile in area, outlying the Walhalla Plateau (itself an outlier of the Kaibab Plateau). François Matthes introduced the mythological conceit of Wotan (chief of the Norse pantheon) presiding over Walhalla (paradisiacal beerhall of Viking heroes fallen in battle) in his U.S. Geological Survey map of 1905. In 1937, the American Museum of Natural History in New York dispatched a team to Wotan's Throne to investigate faunal insularity. The garishly-named little mesa was ballyhooed in the press as a "sky island" sanctuary for anachronistic species — dinosaurs, maybe! Although the museum team scaled Wotan's Throne with great show of heroism, Wotan failed to reward it at the top with Doomsday giants or any biological oddities at all. Its only interesting discovery was of some Anasazi ruins — proving that prehistoric human beings negotiated the 400-foot-high Redwall Limestone cliffs as casually as other species.

PHOTOGRAPH BY JEFF GNASS

WOTAN'S THRONE, LOOKING SOUTH-WEST FROM CAPE ROYAL (SUNRISE, SEPTEMBER).

PHOTOGRAPH BY JEFF GNASS

**WOTAN'S THRONE, LOOKING SOUTH-
WEST FROM CAPE ROYAL (FOGGY).**
PHOTOGRAPH BY JACK W. DYKINGA

CAPE ROYAL CLIFFS, LOOKING SOUTHEAST TO
VISHNU TEMPLE FROM CAPE ROYAL (7,865 FEET).
PHOTOGRAPH BY JACK W. DYKINGA

VISHNU TEMPLE (CENTER LEFT), WOTAN'S
THRONE, WALHALLA PLATEAU (CENTER),
AND UNKAR CANYON (RIGHT), LOOKING
NORTHWEST FROM LIPAN POINT, SOUTH
RIM (AUGUST, MORNING). Unkar Canyon, on
the right bank of the "Big Bend" in the Colorado
River, is underlain by the Dox Formation, one of the
Unkar Group of the Precambrian Grand Canyon
Supergroup. The Dox Formation, dominantly silt-
stone and mudstone, erodes readily to broad valleys
and rounded hills.

PHOTOGRAPH BY TOM TILL

VISHNU TEMPLE AND WALHALLA PLATEAU, LOOKING NORTH FROM MORAN POINT, SOUTH RIM (JANUARY, SUNRISE). On clearest days, the visual range from 7,141-foot-high Moran Point is 243 miles. Clarity was not prized, however, by Thomas Moran, the English painter after whom this panoramic point was named. Moran subordinated rocks to clouds in his treatment of the Western landscape. Both as a member of Powell's 1873 North Rim expedition and of Dutton's 1879 survey, Moran rendered the Grand Canyon as a vessel for the foggy atmospheric effects beloved of homesick Englishmen. Even on his paintings worked up from photographs of cloudless Western landscapes, Moran plasters massive banks of clouds. Moran's Turnerian aesthetic dictated that the stark linearity of the Grand Canyon's stratigraphy, so crisply penciled by Holmes for Dutton's survey, be airbrushed out. As though to redress a century later its purchase and hanging in the Capitol of Moran's fuzzy *The Chasm of the Colorado* (1874), the U.S. Congress in 1970 passed the Clean Air Act. Beginning in 1991, phased enforcement of the amended Act by the EPA with respect to the coal-burning Navajo Generating Station, near the Glen Canyon Dam, promises to reduce fractionally the regional air pollution that has more and more wrapped the real Grand Canyon in Moran's pictorial gauze.

PHOTOGRAPH BY RANDY PRENTICE

VISHNU TEMPLE, LOOKING NORTHWEST FROM LIPAN POINT (MORNING). As doomed as Gunga Din, a last brave flourish of Kaibab Limestone (7,533 feet) trumpets atop Vishnu Temple, the farthest outlier of the Walhalla Plateau. Clarence Dutton wrote in his *Tertiary History of the Grand Cañon District* (1882): "The eye is at once caught by an object which seems to surpass in beauty anything we have yet seen. It is a gigantic butte, so admirably designed and so exquisitely decorated that the sight of it must call forth an expression of wonder and delight from the most apathetic beholder. Its summit is more than 5,000 feet above the river. Mr. Holmes' picture will convey a much more accurate idea of it than any verbal description can possibly do. We named it VISHNU'S TEMPLE."

PHOTOGRAPH BY TOM TILL

CHUAR SEGMENT

T HE CHUAR morphological segment of the Grand Canyon extends twenty-four river miles from the eastern end of the Upper Granite Gorge at Mile 77 to Little Nankoweap Creek at Mile 52. Within the Chuar segment, the East Kaibab Monocline virtually coincides with the Butte Fault along a northerly strike.

On the Butte Fault, one of the array of north-trending Precambrian basement normal faults, the western block dropped 10,000 feet around 820 million years ago. Erosional leveling of the Precambrian structures produced Powell's Great Unconformity in the Grand Canyon between the Precambrian rocks and the overlying Paleozoic strata. The Great Unconformity devoured a two-mile thick sequence of Late Precambrian sedimentary strata everywhere except for some isolated remnants in the Grand Canyon east of Mile 135 (most extensively in the Chuar segment), where stratal wedges took sanctuary in the deep angles, or *half-grabens*, formed by the dropped blocks against principal normal faults. During the Laramide reactivation of the Precambrian normal faults as a reverse faults, the western block was uplifted 2,700 feet on the Butte Fault. This displacement was expressed in the hitherto flat veneer of Paleozoic strata as the East Kaibab Monocline, stepping down to the east by the same 2,700 feet. Net displacement of Precambrian rocks on the hangingwall of Butte Fault is therefore thousands of feet *downward*, even though the directly overlying Paleozoic strata are displaced 2,700 feet *upward*.

The geometrical superposition of the East Kaibab Monocline on the Butte Fault determines which rocks crop out along the Colorado River in the Chuar segment. The southern half of the channel of the Colorado River through the Chuar segment of the Grand Canyon cuts a "Big Bend" across the upper limb of the East Kaibab Monocline transversely (east-west) and exposes at its core the oldest (1.3 to 1.0 billion years) and some of the rarest sedimentary formations in the Grand Canyon region: the northeast-tilted Precambrian Unkar Group of the Grand Canyon Supergroup.

The northern half of the channel of the Colorado River through the Chuar segment cuts along the lower limb of the East Kaibab Monocline longitudinally (north-south), running parallel to base of the monocline in the same manner as we saw in lower Havasu Canyon. This northern half of the Colorado River channel in the Chuar segment exposes the much younger Paleozoic strata that are ubiquitous in the Grand Canyon region.

VIEW NORTHEAST FROM SOUTH RIM PAST SINKING SHIP (LEFT), CORONADO BUTTE , MORAN POINT (RIGHT) TO THE PALISADES OF THE DESERT (OCTOBER, DUSK). All the features named are capped by Kaibab Limestone.
PHOTOGRAPH BY JEFF GNASS

The loftiest rimline of the Grand Canyon, intersecting the southeastern flank of the Kaibab Dome, rises from Cape Final (7,865 feet) north to Point Imperial (8,819 feet). Midway down the declivity from this rimline to the northern half of the channel of the Colorado River through the Chuar segment, the Chuar Group of the Grand Canyon Supergroup lies exposed on the west side of Butte Fault. Younger (1.0 to 0.8 billion years old) than the Unkar Group, the Chuar Group includes in its upper section formations deposited at the same time that the western block was being downthrown, so that these formations were dragged into a marginal concavity or *syncline*.

The right and left banks of the Chuar segment display strong asymmetry in the same general sense as do the North and South Rims in the Kaibab segment. On the right bank, the 6,000-foot relief between the snowy North Rim and the Colorado River drives the high erosive potential of long tributaries that radiate down the eastern flank of the Kaibab Dome, even though unfavorable stratal dip has rendered them intermittent. The soft shales of the Galeros Formation in the Chuar Group erode preferentially to open broad valleys in the northern half of the Chuar segment. The soft siltstones and mudstones of the Dox Formation in the Unkar Group occupy an analogous place in the topography of the southern half of the Chuar segment.

The left bank of the Chuar segment, by contrast, rises precipitously to the Painted Desert on the Marble Platform by cliffs called the Palisades of the Desert and the Desert Façade south and north, respectively, of the confluence with the Grand Canyon's biggest tributary, the Little Colorado River. Apart from the Little Colorado River Gorge, which antedates the Grand Canyon, the left-bank cliffs of the Chuar segment boast remarkably clean, unpunctuated, uncorrugated lines. Lacking appreciable run-off from the desert platform in which the strata dip east and south away from the Grand Canyon, the few short, weak, ephemeral streams of the left bank have made little inroad against the resistant Paleozoic strata of the cliffs. Only in the southern half of the Chuar segment do canyons push back on the left bank, because the shales of the Dox Formation outcropping on both sides of the river there are so readily eroded.

HILLTOP RUINS (LEFT BANK, MILE 71), LOOKING WEST TO FREYA CASTLE, VISHNU TEMPLE, RAMA SHRINE, AND THE TABERNACLE ON SKYLINE (JULY). We are standing on Dox Formation rock near Cardenas Creek. These Anasazi ruins were discovered by Robert Stanton's expedition in 1890. PHOTOGRAPH BY TOM TILL

COLORADO RIVER BENEATH PALISADES OF THE DESERT, LOOKING
NORTHEAST FROM NEAR HILLTOP RUIN (LEFT BANK, MILE 71) (JULY).
PHOTOGRAPH BY TOM TILL

The Little Colorado River, a stream originating over 200 miles to the southeast near the New Mexican border, runs a course parallel to and some thirty miles inboard of the Mogollon Rim, the southwestern border of the Colorado Plateau. It flows to this day in a northwest-trending strike-valley (or *cuesta trough*), under the same stratigraphic control that governed the course of the ancestral upper Colorado River across the Arizona Strip. This trough is formed by the angle between the resistant Kaibab Limestone bed and the overlying Mesozoic erosional scarp, a hard-over-soft couplet of Shinarump Conglomerate over Moenkopi mudstone.

For millions of years, the valley of the Little Colorado River has been migrating northeastward as the basal Mesozoic scarp has eroded back down the northeastward slope of the Colorado Plateau. This migration has scored a *moiré* pattern of gravel-lined fossil channels into the Kaibab Limestone substrate. On the approach to its confluence with the Colorado River in the depths of the Grand Canyon, the modern Little Colorado River has incised itself right down to the lowest Paleozoic stratum, the Tapeats Sandstone.

On the south bank of the Little Colorado River a mile upstream from its confluence with the Colorado River, on August 11, 1869, Captain Powell's party discovered potsherd-littered ruins. In February, 1890, a prospector named Ben Beamer moved into these ruins, where he improvised a shelter and gallantly tilled the alluvial soil.

Beamer was not the first person to opportunize the prehistoric ghost-towns of the Grand Canyon. In the middle of the twelfth century, the Kayenta Anasazi, who had extensively colonized the eastern Grand Canyon region from river to rim, began a folk-migration 100 miles east across the Painted Desert to the Hopi Mesas. At the foot of the third Hopi Mesa is the Old Oraibi pueblo, founded about 1150 AD; it is the oldest continuously-occupied town in the United States. Soon after the completion by the close of the thirteenth century of the Anasazi exodus, Paiute nomads began straggling into the Grand Canyon from the north to live it up in abandoned Anasazi sites such as the Nankoweap ruins.

Beamer had, however, the unwitting distinction of squatting on one of the few Hopi (post-Anasazi Pueblo) sites in the Grand Canyon. Later investigation revealed that the potsherd assemblage reported by Powell's party includes early Hopi yellow-ware in addition to the older Anasazi black-on-white and gray ceramic. Sacred sites near the mouth of the Little Colorado River are so central to Hopi (and formerly, by inference, to Anasazi) notions of their phylogenesis that they continue to be the objects of pilgrimage by modern Hopi. A centuries-old ceremonial trail beginning at the Hopi Mesas leads to a site a few miles upstream of Beamer's Cabin called Sipapu.

VIEW NORTHEAST FROM DESERT VIEW
OVER THE PALISADES OF THE DESERT
TO ECHO CLIFFS ON SKYLINE (LATE
AFTERNOON).
PHOTOGRAPH BY LARRY ULRICH

Sipapu is a bright yellow spring ten feet across that pierces a travertine dome at the foot of the limestone cliffs. The Hopi religion identifies this dome as the antechamber to the Earth's interior. The ancestors of human beings and animals rose through three rather unpleasant underworlds and then, as it were, decompressed in this archetypal *kiva* (underground ceremonial chamber) before surfacing in the sublunary world. *Kachinas* (spirits of dead people, animals and plants) slip through the aperture of Sipapu back into the Earth, whence they may be persuaded by the prayers of living Hopi to return seasonally as beneficent rainclouds. The Hopi ceremonial trail, worn on top of the bank of Tapeats Sandstone, continues past Sipapu four miles west to the confluence of the Little Colorado and Colorado Rivers; then winds two miles south on the left bank of the Colorado River, past the blending of the parallel ribbons of warm brown Little Colorado and cold green Colorado waters, to the Sacred Hopi Salt Mines. These evaporite deposits, leached from Tapeats Sandstone, provide sacramental table salt for Hopi rituals.

MT. HAYDEN, LOOKING SOUTHEAST FROM POINT IMPE-RIAL PAST COLTER BUTTE (CENTER RIGHT), GUNTHER'S CASTLE, AND CHUAR BUTTE TO THE LITTLE COLORADO RIVER GORGE AND CAPE SOLITUDE. We are standing on the Kaibab Limestone of Point Imperial (formerly, Skidoo Point), at 8,819 feet the highest viewpoint on the rim of the Grand Canyon. We are looking at Coconino Sandstone-capped Mount Hayden (8,362 feet), named for Carl Hayden, the Arizona congressman who was instrumental in engineering the establishment of Grand Canyon National Park in 1919. Beyond Mount Hayden appear successively the lower Supai Group-capped Colter Butte, Gunther's Castle, and a valley underlain by Precambrian Chuar Group rocks that are truncated by the Butte Fault. On the upthrown side of the Butte Fault rises the Kaibab Limestone-capped Chuar Butte (6,394 feet).

PHOTOGRAPH BY DAVID MUENCH

BEAMER'S CABIN, LEFT BANK OF THE LITTLE COLORADO
RIVER ONE MILE FROM THE CONFLUENCE WITH THE
COLORADO RIVER.
PHOTOGRAPH BY FRED HIRSCHMANN

CHUAR BUTTE, LOOKING WEST FROM THE RIGHT
BANK OF LITTLE COLORADO RIVER NEAR THE
CONFLUENCE WITH THE COLORADO RIVER.
PHOTOGRAPH BY LARRY ULRICH

VIEW FROM VISTA ENCANTADA (NORTH RIM, 8456 FEET), LOOKING NORTHEAST
PAST BRADY PEAK, ALSAP BUTTE, AND NOVINGER BUTTE; NANKOWEAP MESA
(RIGHT); DESERT FACADE; TO THUNDERSTORM OVER THE MARBLE PLATFORM
AND ECHO CLIFFS ON SKYLINE (AUGUST, AFTERNOON).

PHOTOGRAPH BY JACK W. DYKINGA

RIM FLORA

BLADDERPOD IN HAIL, NORTH RIM.
PHOTOGRAPH BY TOM TILL

**ASPEN AND PONDEROSA PINE,
NEAR POINT IMPERIAL.**
PHOTOGRAPH BY JACK W. DYKINGA

Walhalla Plateau was called "Greenland Plateau" before François Matthes re-christened it. This Dutch-born geologist, in his 1902-1905 campaign to map the topography of the Grand Canyon for the U.S. Geological Survey with greater accuracy than Dutton had attempted, followed the practice of his predecessor (who was trained in divinity before joining Powell's survey) in concocting kitschy place-names from a grab-bag of exotic religions.

The original name was decidedly more descriptive, insofar as the "coastal" outlines of the Walhalla Plateau and Greenland as well as the "off-shore" position of each "island" relative to its "mainland" are suggestively similar. The Walhalla Plateau is a big southeastern outlier of the Kaibab Plateau, stranded in the Grand Canyon by the headward erosion of Bright Angel Canyon as it chases the Bright Angel Fault upcountry across the Kaibab Plateau. From an elevation of 8,500 feet at the head of Bright Angel Canyon, the Walhalla Plateau drops across a distance of eight miles to 7,800 feet at its southern rim.

This topographic elevational interval, determined by the one-degree dip to the southwest of the Paleozoic strata on the southern flank of the Kaibab Dome, overlaps another elevational interval between 8,250 and 7,000 feet that is identified as the *Transition Zone* in C. Hart Merriam's classic plant-distribution scheme. This scheme, based on the naturalist's 1889 fieldwork in northern Arizona, postulates that continental species-zonations (called *life zones*) corresponding to broad latitudinal belts are, to a first approximation, recapitulated by local life zones corresponding to narrow elevational belts. The following sequence of life zones, in order of decreasing elevation and increasing temperature, is typically present throughout Grand Canyon National Park: Boreal, Transition, Upper Sonoran, Lower Sonoran. The Transition Zone is dominated by ponderosa pine, generally in nearly pure stands only slightly admixed with Gambel oak and mountain-mahogany or fringed by aspen.

Ponderosa pine, true to Merriam's prediction, covers most of the Walhalla Plateau. On the "coastal" areas of the Kaibab Plateau "mainland," ponderosa pine is common but far from universal. Where erosion of the Kaibab Plateau has removed the elevation interval corresponding to the Transition Zone from the plateau-top to the cliffside (as it has in Bright Angel Canyon), the Boreal Zone is found to abut the Upper Sonoran instead of grading into the Transition Zone. In such areas, Boreal spruce and fir forest sweeps down the plateau flush to the rim and abruptly yields the subjacent slope to Upper Sonoran pinyon-juniper woodland.

Walhalla Plateau's noble tracts of ponderosa pine represent the forest that would—but for the accident of the intervening ditch—vault Bright Angel Canyon and soar on its nine-inch-needle carpet unopposed to the South Rim.

ASPENS, PINES, SPRUCE.
PHOTOGRAPH BY WILLIAM NEILL

ASPENS BY GREENLAND LAKE,
WALHALLA PLATEAU.
PHOTOGRAPH BY LARRY ULRICH

PURPLE LOBELIA IN ASPEN-LINED MEADOW, KAIBAB PLATEAU.
PHOTOGRAPH BY JAMES RANDKLEV

PONDEROSA PINES NEAR LIPAN POINT.
PHOTOGRAPH BY STEVE MULLIGAN

MARBLE CANYON SEGMENT

THE MARBLE morphological segment of the Grand Canyon extends from Little Nankoweap Creek at Mile 52 to Lees Ferry at Mile 0. The Colorado River in the Marble segment is contained in Marble Canyon. Marble Canyon is a comparatively straight, steep-walled gash from Mile 62 northeastward to Mile 0 across the flat, lowlying, Kaibab Limestone-capped Marble Platform.

The Paleozoic formations intersected by the Colorado River at the bottom of Marble Canyon are progressively younger upriver. Going northeast up Marble Canyon, each of the formations in the Grand Canyon's stack of Paleozoic strata successively disappears in stratigraphically-upward order: Tapeats Sandstone slips from view at River Mile 58; Bright Angel Shale, at Mile 47; Muav Limestone, at Mile 37; Redwall Limestone, at Mile 23; Lower Supai Group, at Mile 15; Esplanade Sandstone, at Mile 11; Hermit Shale, at Mile 5; Coconino Sandstone, at Mile 4.5; Toroweap Formation, at Mile 2; last of all, Kaibab Limestone disappears at Mile 0.7.

The steep gradient of the Colorado River between Miles 62 and 0 (8.2 feet per mile) contributes to this northward-younging effect at river's edge. Quantitatively, though, gradient accounts for only a fifth of the observed stratigraphic displacement.

The chief cause of the northward-younging phenomenon is the northeastward dip (less than one degree on average) of the Paleozoic strata on the Marble Platform. Of the physiographic units in the Grand Canyon region, the Marble Platform has been least compromised by the encroachments of the Basin and Range province insofar as it is farthest removed from the tectonic transition zone. It best preserves, therefore, that ancient regional slope, declining northeast from the Mogollon Highlands, that controlled the northwestward course of the ancestral upper Colorado River downstream of the Kaibab Dome.

Marble Canyon, by virtue of the antecedent antiquity of the ancestral upper Colorado River, cuts across the grain of the prevailing structural slope. Structural slope is down to the northeast; Marble Canyon is down to the southwest. Tributaries in the Marble segment, by contrast, enjoy no historical dispensation from the laws of gravity. North of the influence of the Kaibab Dome (north, that is, of Mile 52), ephemeral desert streams flow down the northeastward structural slope, intersecting the southwest-flowing Colorado River at acute angles pointing upriver (*barbed angles*). The side canyons of the Marble segment are correspondingly barbed, short, and steep.

NANKOWEAP RUINS (RIGHT BANK, MILE 53), LOOKING SOUTH-EAST (JUNE). These Anasazi ruins, perched 400 precarious feet above the Colorado River on a Muav Limestone cliff, may have been granaries for crops grown in the alluvium at the mouth of Nankoweap Canyon.

PHOTOGRAPH BY TOM TILL

Northeastward tilt reduces the elevation of the Kaibab Limestone surface by 2,900 feet between Mile 62 and Mile 0. As Marble Canyon cuts obliquely against this tilt, the depth of Marble Canyon decreases smoothly northeastward. At Mile 62, the entire Paleozoic sequence is displayed in the 3,300-foot-high canyon walls. At Mile 44, the canyon walls are 2,775 feet high; at Mile 21, 1,415 feet; at Mile 8, 465 feet.

Just below Mile 0, the Grand Canyon vanishes to zero. The stratigraphic thickness of the Paleozoic sequence on the Marble Platform (3,300 feet) equals the sum of the elevation differentials between Miles 62 and 0 for the Kaibab Limestone (2,900 feet) and the river (400 feet). Brute geometry determines that, at Mile 0 (to be precise, Mile 0.7), the last bright sliver of Kaibab Limestone must dive into chthonic darkness beneath basal Mesozoic mudstone. The overlying mile-thick pile of Mesozoic strata forms the Grand Staircase of Mesozoic hard-over-soft couplets that, starting in this neighborhood with the Vermilion and Echo Cliffs, steps up out of the Grand Canyon region and into Utah.

It is fitting that we take our leave of the Grand Canyon's caprock at Mile 0. If we had arranged to pop out at Mile 278 instead, we would now be facing a dreary finality. To the west and south of the Grand Canyon's mouth, the Kaibab Limestone is gone forever, annihilated in the Laramide unconformity. To the north and east of the Grand Canyon's head, the Kaibab Limestone present and has a promising, if distant, future. There the Kaibab Limestone has gone safely to the ground, not to be exhumed for ages still to come.

When and how to be exhumed, who can know? Some whisper of a kachina, brooding under the Grand Staircase, who will emerge as the next Grand Canyon. He is prepared to wait an eon, until the first Grand Canyon has flitted back down through Sipapu.

VIEW FROM TATAHATSO POINT OVER PRESIDENT HARDING RAPIDS (LEFT BANK, MILE 44), LOOKING SOUTHWEST PAST POINT HANSBROUGH AND THE MARBLE PLATFORM TO THE KAIBAB PLATEAU ON THE SYKLINE. The entrenched meander of Point Hansbrough is composed of Muav and Redwall Limestone capped by Supai Group rocks. The Marble Platform and adjoining Kaibab Plateau are, despite their 3,000-foot elevation difference, both capped by the same Kaibab Limestone stratum. The whole sequence of Paleozoic strata is stepped down these 3,000 feet to the east by the East Kaibab Monocline. Erosion gnawing at the hinge of the monocline has exposed Toroweap Formation and Coconino Sandstone (seen in this photograph as the thin orangish band) below the Kaibab Limestone.

Point Hansbrough is named for Peter Hansbrough, who drowned here on Robert Stanton's ill-starred 1889 expedition to survey the route for a proposed Denver-to-San Diego railroad via the Grand Canyon. Hansbrough had five days earlier scratched on Esplanade Sandstone at Mile 12 the epitaph for Frank Brown, president of the railroad company, who drowned there in Brown's Riffle. President Brown had disdained to supply Stanton's expedition with such effeminate appurtenances as life preservers. President Harding Rapids commemorate the death of another president. The 1923 U.S. Geological Survey party laid over a day here to solemnize President Harding's funeral.

PHOTOGRAPH BY TOM TILL

VIEW FROM TATAHATSO POINT (LEFT BANK, MILE 43)
SOUTH ACROSS POINT HANSBROUGH (RIGHT BANK) TO
SASE NASKET (LEFT BANK, MILE 47). Both Tatahatso Point (on
which we and the agave are standing) and Sase Nasket promontory with
adjacent pillar in the distance are capped by Kaibab Limestone.

PHOTOGRAPH BY CARR CLIFTON

MUAV AND REDWALL LIMESTONE IN THE WALLS OF BUCK FARM CANYON (RIGHT BANK, MILE 41). The contact between these two limestone formations is inconspicuous because their layering is parallel and they are alike stained red by the overlying redbeds of the Supai Group formations. The contact between Late Cambrian Muav Limestone and Middle Mississippian Redwall Limestone corresponds, nevertheless, to 180 million years of missing history. Lenses of impure Temple Butte Limestone at the top of the Muav Limestone, well-exposed in Buck Farm Canyon, represent Middle Devonian channel-infill that survived the Late Devonian peneplanation that removed an unknown thickness of superjacent Temple Butte Limestone. In the missing history between the Muav Limestone's first emergence (the Muav/Temple Butte contact) and second emergence (the Muav/Redwall contact), land plants made their appearance.

PHOTOGRAPH BY TOM TILL

SACRED DATURA, Also known as jimsonweed, sacred datura *(Datura meteloides)* is an hallucinogenic member of the Deadly Nightshade Family. From August to October, its tubular flowers bloom white at night but turn purple after dawn.

PHOTOGRAPH BY TOM TILL

VASEY'S PARADISE, MARBLE CANYON (RIGHT BANK, MILE 32) (JUNE). Powell named Vasey's Paradise in 1869 for a botanist who had accompanied him the year before on an excursion to the upper Colorado River drainage. The several springs that irrigate this hanging garden foam from caves high on the Redwall Limestone walls above the Colorado River. G.W. Vasey's tongue would surely have hung out at the helleborine orchids, yellow and crimson monkeyflowers, and maidenhair ferns served on a bed of watercress, squaw bush, and poison ivy. Too bad that Vasey never glimpsed his eponymous Paradise and that squaw bush stinks.

Perversely, there is no marble in Marble Canyon. The misnomer was the fault of a future director of the U.S. Geological Survey. Although by 1869 he had already been a professor of geology at Illinois Wesleyan University, John Wesley Powell mistook river-polish on the Redwall Limestone of Marble Canyon for metamorphism.

PHOTOGRAPH BY TOM TILL

HOOKER EVENING PRIMROSE, MARBLE CANYON. Found only in the Inner Gorge, the Hooker evening primrose (*Oenothera hookeri*) is a biennial that blooms July-September. Each flower blooms white for just one night, turns orange-red at the dawn, then wilts into the day.
PHOTOGRAPH BY LARRY ULRICH

VIEW OF MARBLE CANYON UPSTREAM
FROM NORTH CANYON RAPID (MILE 20.6).
PHOTOGRAPH BY LARRY ULRICH

**VIEW OF MARBLE CANYON DOWNSTREAM
FROM MOUTH OF NORTH CANYON (RIGHT
BANK, MILE 20.6).**

PHOTOGRAPH BY LARRY ULRICH

MARBLE CANYON: AERIAL VIEW NORTHEAST FROM ABOVE NORTH CANYON PAST HOT NA NA WASH ON THE MARBLE PLATFORM TO ECHO CLIFFS AND NAVAJO MOUNTAIN ON THE ARIZONA-UTAH BORDER (OCTOBER, SUNSET).

PHOTOGRAPH BY JEFF GNASS

VERMILION CLIFFS, LOOKING WEST OVER MAR-
BLE CANYON (MAY, SUNRISE).

PHOTOGRAPH BY CARR CLIFTON

**SLICKROCK POOLS IN NORTH CANYON (RIGHT
BANK, MILE 20).** North Canyon, descending northeast
into south-descending Marble Canyon, displays the *barbed*
morphology that characterizes side canyons in the Marble
segment of the Grand Canyon. At Mile 20, Marble Canyon
cuts down through Kaibab Limestone and Hermit Shale into
the Supai Group. North Canyon joins Marble Canyon by a
narrow, steep, and high-walled cleft in the Supai Group.
The slickrock pools in the photograph have formed in the
Esplanade Sandstone Member, uppermost of the Supai
Group. The smooth, curving walls are exfoliation features
of the sandstone.

PHOTOGRAPH BY FRED HIRSCHMANN

BEAVERTAIL CACTUS (LEFT BANK, MILE 4), LOOKING NORTH UP MARBLE CANYON TO PARIA CANYON (CENTER) AND VERMILION CLIFFS (LEFT). We are standing on Kaibab Limestone. Coconino Sandstone is the river-level formation here.

Although beavertail cactus (*Opuntia basilaris*) is the only spineless cactus in the Grand Canyon region, it is not innocuous. One must still beware its *glochids* (tiny tufted barbs). It blooms March-May.

PHOTOGRAPH BY DAVID MUENCH

BADGER CREEK RAPID (MILE 8) AND VERMILION CLIFFS ON SKYLINE, LOOK-
ING SOUTHWEST (DOWNSTREAM) FROM JACKASS CANYON (LEFT BANK) (JUNE
SUNRISE).   The capstone is, as usual, Kaibab Limestone.   Toroweap Formation and Coconino
Sandstone make up the steep canyon walls.   Hermit Shale peeps out at river-level.

PHOTOGRAPH BY TOM TILL

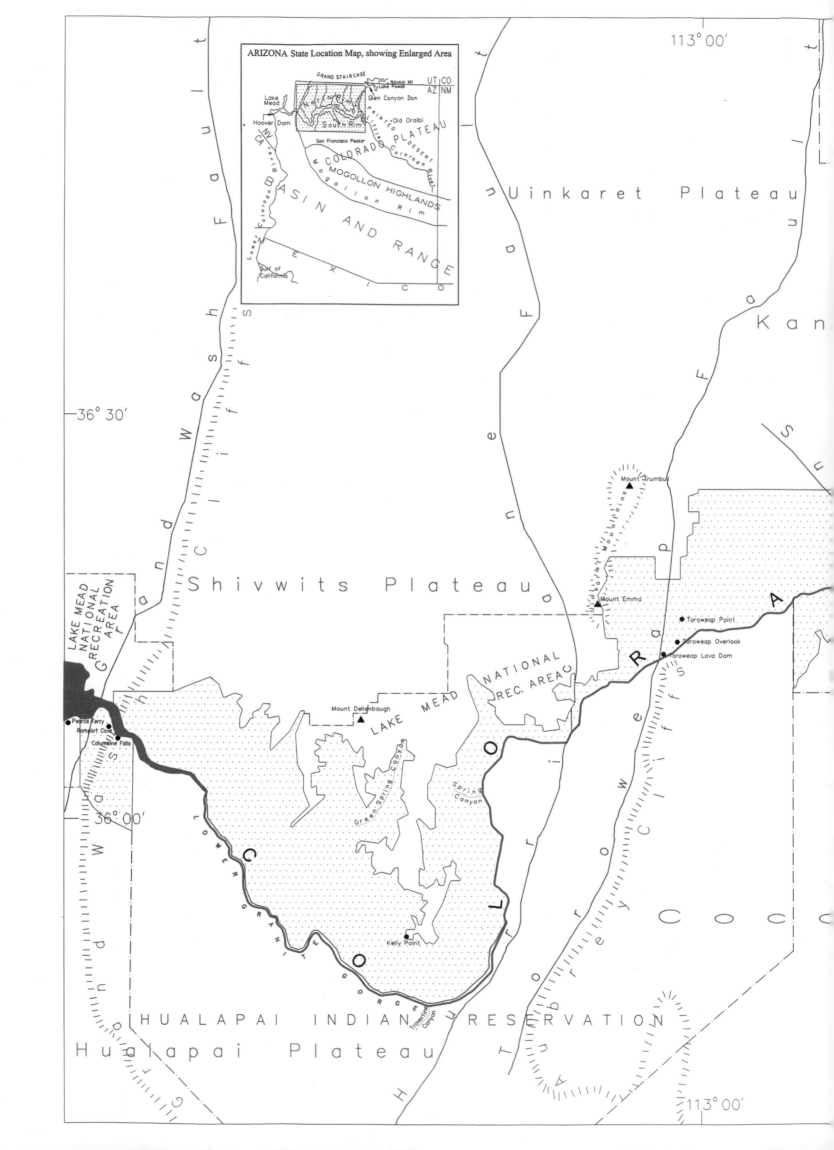

ARIZONA State Location Map, showing Enlarged Area

GRAND STAIRCASE
Navajo Mt
UT CO
Lake Powell
AZ NM
Glen Canyon Dam
Lake
Mead
Old Oraibi
Hoover Dam
San Francisco Peaks
COLORADO PLATEAU
PAINTED DESERT
Little Colorado River
MOGOLLON HIGHLANDS
Mogollon Rim
BASIN AND RANGE
Gulf of California

Uinkaret Plateau

Kan

Shivwits Plateau

Mount Trumbull

Uinkaret Mountains

Mount Emma

Toroweap Point

Toroweap Overlook

Toroweap Lava Dam

Mount Dellenbaugh

LAKE MEAD NATIONAL REC. AREA

LAKE MEAD NATIONAL RECREATION AREA

Pearce Ferry
Rampart Cave
Columbine Falls

Green Spring Canyon

Spring Canyon

Kelly Point

HUALAPAI INDIAN RESERVATION

Hualapai Plateau

36° 30'

36° 00'